D1145935

The ups & downs of being a HUSBAND

The ups & downs of being a HUSBAND

Tony Husband

ARCTURUS

Thanks to Private Eye for very kindly allowing us to use their cartoons.

The cartoons on pages 6, 10, 14, 17, 18, 27, 45, 48, 63, 67, 69, 70, 74, 77, 81, 83, 84, 86, 88, 90, 96, 97, 103, 104, 116, 117 are reproduced by kind permission of *PRIVATE EYE* magazine/Tony Husband – www.private-eye.co.uk

ARCTURUS

This edition published in 2016 by Arcturus Publishing Limited
26/27 Bickels Yard, 151–153 Bermondsey Street,
London SE1 3HA

Copyright © Arcturus Holdings Limited/Tony Husband

All rights reserved. No part of this publication may be reproduced, stored in a retrieval system, or transmitted, in any form or by any means, electronic, mechanical, photocopying, recording or otherwise, without prior written permission in accordance with the provisions of the Copyright Act 1956 (as amended). Any person or persons who do any unauthorised act in relation to this publication may be liable to criminal prosecution and civil claims for damages.

ISBN: 978-1-78428-382-7
AD005374UK

Printed in China

INTRODUCTION

As a husband and as a Husband, I should be in a prime position to talk about being a husband. I'm not sure I am, though, after all these years. I'm still flummoxed by it.

Marriage, it seems, is a series of compromises; it has to be to be successful. There has to be a lot of biting one's tongue and, while we're at it, a whole series of sorrys, getting down off one's high horse and a certain amount of grovelling.

Marriage is the frontline in the battle of the sexes, where what should be a team game can often become over-competitive and a breeding ground for resentment. We don't always understand each other too well, do we? For example, a husband might tell his wife 'I've got a surprise for you' and turn up with a heavy pack and a tent on his back for a camping holiday in the Brecon Beacons when what she really wants is to be whisked off to a five-star hotel in Paris or New York. It doesn't end there. A week later, she might have fixed up to have dinner with the Blenkinsops on the actual night of the World Cup final. This stuff goes on and on.

In marriage some men who were once perfectly capable of looking after themselves mysteriously lose their skills at operating the oven/iron/washing machine. That doesn't stop them from playing on the X-box at the age of 40-plus; it's the perfect way of putting off all the DIY work they've promised to do.

They say elephants never forget but in my experience it's wives. It all goes down on the record. Wives have supernatural powers to read husbands' minds. Be warned: if you ever do anything wrong, your wife will know. They always find out. It's one of life's great certainties.

I hope you recognize some of the situations in these cartoons. They do happen.

Tony Husband

'Oh well, another day, another pair of underpants...'

'Do I love you? Yes... Do I love you more than United?
Now you're being silly.'

'Darling, please don't leave. How will I manage without you?'

'I worry that Les misses the cut and thrust of business since he retired.'

'The daft thing is, *we've* loads of cheese in the fridge.'

'Oh dear, bad day at work, dear?'

'He's trained the cat to hide his bald patch.'

'Why don't you just go for a swim like everyone else?'

'You should get your wife to shave your back. I do.'

'Jill, what time's my wife's funeral?'

'Milly... she's alive.'

'You must admit the damp has its benefits...
We're saving on furniture.'

'Right, dear, are you all belted-up ready for my latest home brew?'

'Oh, for crying out loud, Peter, grow up.'

'He's very possessive with her...'

'OK, do you find me: a. Sexy?; b. Very sexy?; c. Irresistible?...'

'Shhhh...hic...'

'For goodness sake, Barry, not that every time
Mother comes around.'

'Darling, I like your husband,
but there's something strange about him.'

26

'I'm your wife, Jeremy. I've every right to know
where you go at night.'

'Drink? No thanks, I'm with my husband... he's playing darts.'

'Yes, very impressive, dear, but when do you start on your legs?'

'My husband's a bit paranoid about drones.'

'You'll have to excuse my husband. He's not very sociable.'

'Water tank? No, it's my husband's beer supply.'

'It's my wife, doctor. She seems very tense.'

'Where's the car? Erm, do you remember when I said I'd got a rare chance of getting a season ticket for United?'

'I say, would you stop shouting like that?
My wife's got a dreadful headache.'

'Sorry about this. My husband was reared by baboons.'

'And where do you think you're going?'

'Ignore him. He's sulking because I said he couldn't open
any wine until you came.'

'C'mon, Walter. Can't we share a car like everyone else?'

'Can you call back? He's on mole watch.'

'Last time I'm telling you, Tom...
There are children waiting to have a go.'

'When's my wife having the baby? Erm, should be about now, I think.'

'I told you it was a mistake playing golf with your mother.'

'What on earth did you say in your letter to the Prime Minister?'

'If you're not back in an hour, I'll call the rescue services.'

'Aren't you supposed to take your trousers off first?'

'I should have warned you... Des loves goldfish.'

'It's very nice, but I presumed the pond would be in the garden.'

'I should have said, Michael has a spittoon by his chair at home.'

'John, I respect your ambition to be an escapologist, but you've
been in there for two hours.'

'You're right. My wife has put a camera on the dog's collar.'

'He's saving up for the balloon.'

'Uh oh, my wife's not happy; she's texting me in capitals.'

'For heaven's sake, Peter, it's only an overdue library book.'

'No, literally I'm in the doghouse.'

'We've rung your wife, Graham, she's on her way.'

'Mr Parker, if you want to make this work you need to concentrate.'

'Ah, Joe, isn't it? My wife's had to tell me all about you.'

'I'm childish?!! Huh, you're a million, zillion, billion times more childish than me.'

'Isn't that her from the next apartment?'

'Why don't you get the train to work like everyone else?'

'Oh wow, great!! United are on.'

'Huh, gardens?! Our garden's so big our lawnmower needs a
sat nav, doesn't it, darling?'

'It's no good, I can't sleep. I think I'll practise my trombone.'

'Hello, yes... we think you've installed the television upside down.'

'Oh hi, dear, we were just talking about you.'

'We once had an overdue library book...'

'My wife makes the best dumplings ever.'

'For heaven's sake, George, treat yourself to a sunray lamp.'

'Bill's a night watchman.'

'Tell you what, I'll be glad when the television's repaired.'

'Just a minute... you're not my wife.'

'I know you love trifle, Roger, but so does everybody else.'

'Is it me or are these frozen chickens getting smaller?'

'Did you want to talk about work?'

'The toilet seat's up! Have you had a man in this house?'

'My wife's gone to the gym.'

'Oi, mate, are you not looking at my wife?'

'Joyce, what's this about you and some circus clown?!!'

'You're wanted on the phone.'

'I hate his Errol Flynn Appreciation Society nights.'

'It's the way he stares at other women.'

'Tch... 400 years and they're all as boring as you.'

'Do you remember when we used to go out to enjoy ourselves?'

'Personally I think it's over the top and unnecessary.'

'Yes, it will be all quiet next door.
They're watching you through the window.'

'Ner, ner, ner... ner, ner...'

'Okay. Is Ben a police car, fire engine or ambulance?'

'I'm leaving you, Jess.'

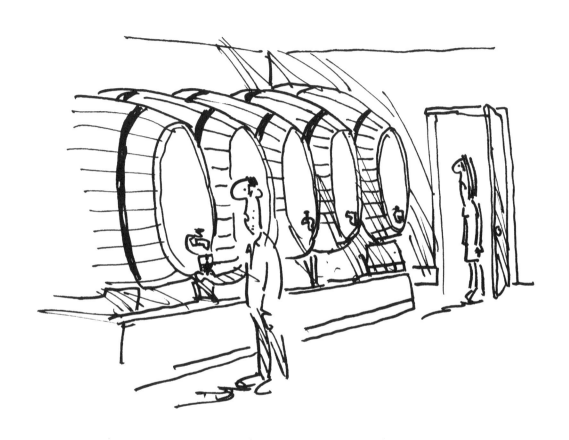

'Did I drink all the wine last night?'

'I told you not to be too critical of him.'

'He got his toe stuck in the tap.'

'He sat down, his wife looked tired, frail, the strains of bringing up four children showed... I'm talking like a novel again, he said -- I can't help it, sorry.'

'Oh cripes... the Holgates are back from their Mexican holiday.'

'I think you over-feed that canary, Roger.'

'Yeah, woke up this morning, got the saw my wife in her curlers blues...'

'I think you may have the wrong idea about fantasy football.'

'My wife said WE have to tighten our belts, so I did.'

'Yes, I'll give you a tip, mate: stop looking down my wife's dress.'

'I've been replaced by a doormat.'

'I've just seen my wife with another man.'

'No, still no signal, darling.'

'Hic, it's my wife asking where I am... good question, where am I?'

'(Sigh) I don't know if my husband's a party animal or partly animal.'

'Dr Livingstone, I presume.'

'John, can we drop the puppet show tonight?'

'Oh no, not woolly mammoth again!!'

'Oh hi, love, brought a couple of friends round to watch the match.'

'Look what I bought at the charity shop!!'

'Our midfield's rubbish. That reminds me,
are we having turkey for lunch?'

'You should get your wife involved in golf. I did!'

'We prefer to stay in, don't we, Darren?'

'I've sorted out the problem with the neighbours.'

'Never mind where it's from. How strong is it?'

'Have I seen the cat? No, I've been too busy laying this carpet.'

'Could you pass the salt, dear?'

'Erm... see you down there, darling.'

'Hi, Phil, it's me darling. I want you back and guess what?
I've won the lottery.'

'Let's go for a leisurely row around the bay, you said.'

'Oh damn, I just remembered, your mother died this morning.'

'Five quid on me losing all my money by the end of the day.'